My Fir
B

By Molly Davidson
Mendon Cottage books

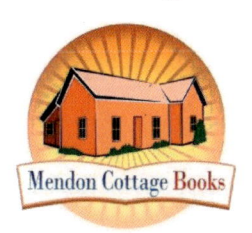

JD-Biz Publishing

Download Free Books!
http://MendonCottageBooks.com

All Rights Reserved.

No part of this publication may be reproduced in any form or by any means, including scanning, photocopying, or otherwise without prior written permission from JD-Biz Corp and http://AmazingAnimalBooks.com.
Copyright © 2015

All Images Licensed by Fotolia, Pixabay, and 123RF

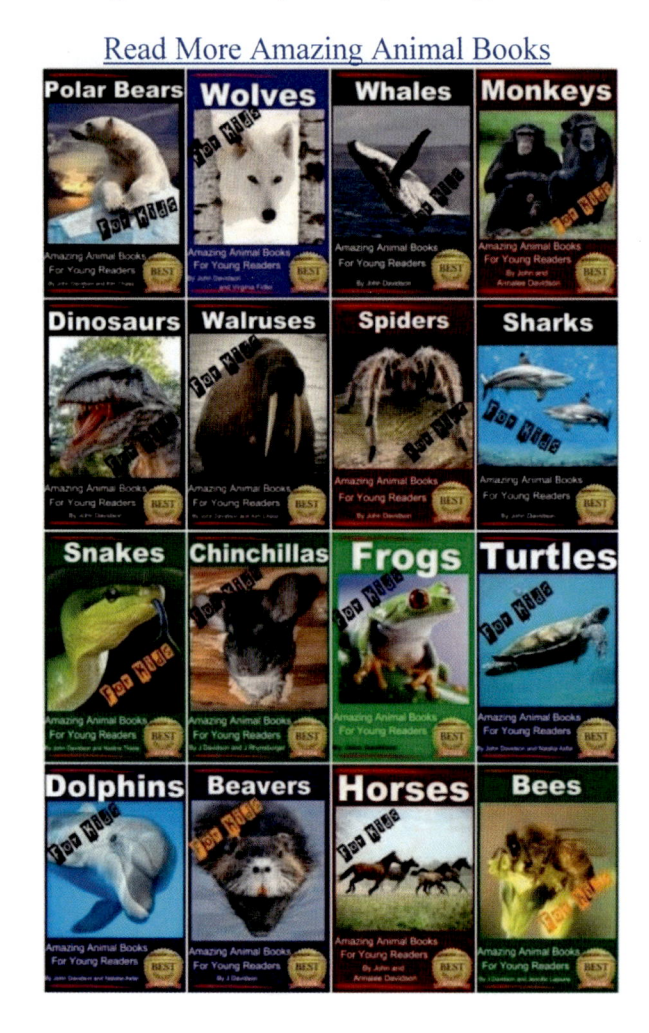

Read More Amazing Animal Books

Download Free Books!
http://MendonCottageBooks.com

Table of Contents

Introduction 4
Butterflies Beautiful Insects 5
Body Parts of a Butterfly 8
Life Cycle of a Butterfly 11
Where Butterflies Live 15
What Do Butterflies Eat? 17
Can Butterflies Communicate? 18
Butterflies and Pollination 19
Butterfly Species 21
Monarch Butterfly and Migration 21
Painted Lady Butterfly 24
Viceroy Butterfly 25
Buckeye One Butterfly 26
Zebra Longwing Butterfly 27
Paper Kite Butterfly 28
Tailed Jay Butterfly 29
Doris Longwing Butterfly 30
Butterfly Meaning in Different Cultures 31
Butterfly Facts 33
Conclusion 35
Publisher 43

Introduction

Did you know that caterpillars turn into butterflies?

Did you know that butterflies fly thousands of miles from one country to another?

Butterflies Beautiful Insects

Their scientific name is Papilionoidea and they belong to the group of Lepidoptera, which means "scaly wings".

Butterflies have a head, thorax (middle part of the body), abdomen (end of the body), two antennae, and six legs.

Butterflies also have four wings covered by colored scales.

Do not touch a butterfly's wings the powder that you see on your hands is actually scales, this damages their wings.

The smallest butterflies are less than one inch wide.

The biggest butterflies reach out to 11 inches.

Butterflies have been on the planet for at least 130 million years.

Butterflies live about one month.

Some butterflies, like the Monarch, Mourning Cloaks, and Tropical Heliconians can live to be 9 months old.

Body Parts of a Butterfly

The life of a butterfly begins as an egg, then a caterpillar, followed by a chrysalis, and finally a butterfly.

Head: It has the eyes, antennae, and brain of the butterfly.

Antennae: The antennae smell for the butterfly and let it know its position.

Labial Palps: Are hair-covered organs that help the butterfly to decide if something is food.

Abdomen: It holds the heart, the digestive system, reproductive organs, and spiracles (breathing holes).

Thorax: The middle section of the butterfly, it holds the wings and legs.

Legs: A butterfly has 6 legs, they can taste food for the butterfly!

Wings: Butterfly's wings are really thin made of a material called chitin (tiny scales). The wings have lots of veins that bring oxygen and blood to them.

Life Cycle of a Butterfly

The life cycle of butterflies is a process in which a caterpillar turns into a beautiful butterfly, it's called metamorphosis.

First stage: A girl adult butterfly lays eggs on a plant. The eggs are very small and round; it takes about five days for the eggs to begin hatching. A tiny green worms hatch from the eggs.

Second stage: The baby caterpillars crawl and the first thing they do is eat the eggshell. After, they eat only leaves and plants from now on.

They grow fast, and have to shed their skin up to five times.

Third stage: A fully-grown caterpillar attaches itself to a twig or a leaf and forms a hard skin known as **chrysalis or pupa.** The caterpillar stops growing and rests. The caterpillar stays like this for two weeks.

Fourth stage: A butterfly comes out of the chrysalis, with wet wings. It takes a few hours for the wings to dry, then the butterfly can fly and goes to find food.

The whole life cycle of a butterfly can last up to a year.

Where Butterflies Live

Butterflies live all over the World, except Antarctica.

Butterflies like warm weather best, some of their favorite places are California, Hawaii, and Mexico.

Butterflies are always moving from place to place, looking for food.

Butterflies don't usually live through the winter, it is too cold.

Monarch butterflies will migrate to a warmer place for the winter.

What Do Butterflies Eat?

Butterflies get their food from drinking.

Butterflies drink nectar from flowers.

They also eat some other things like pollen, rotting fruit, dung, tree sap, and mineral rocks.

Whatever a butterfly eats, is has to be a liquid, so they can drink it.

Can Butterflies Communicate?

Butterflies talk by sound, moving, and by chemicals that are released.

Some butterflies make clicking sounds to protect themselves.

Butterflies cannot hear, so, they feel vibrations.

Butterflies and Pollination

Colorful flowers attract butterflies, so does the smell; they can see bright colors like red, green, and yellow.

Butterflies fly around flowers and gather pollen that sticks to their tiny legs.

When they fly to the next flower, the pollen falls off, then this flower is pollinated, and more flowers can grow.

Butterflies need the flowers for food, and a place to lay their eggs; the flowers need the butterflies to help make new flowers.

Butterfly Species

Monarch Butterfly and Migration

They are very colorful: orange, white, and black.

This coloring is a warning to predators that they are poisonous.

A girl Monarch can lay 400 eggs.

Monarch butterflies have four generations through the year:

The first generation is born in March and April. The second is May and June, and third is July and August.

The first three generations die about 6 weeks after they are born.

The fourth generation is born in September and October. These are the butterflies that migrate. Monarch butterflies don't survive in cold weather. In the winter, they migrate to Mexico, where it is warm.

These butterflies will live until the next spring when they fly north again, and lay their eggs.

Painted Lady Butterfly: It lives in tropical areas with lots of trees.

The Painted Lady Butterfly is mostly black, brown, and orange with some white spots.

Viceroy Butterfly: It lives in the United States, Canada, and Mexico.

The Viceroy Butterfly is dark orange with black lines and a row of white spots on the edge of the wings. It copies the Monarch butterfly.

Buckeye One Butterfly: This butterfly lives in the U.S., Canada, and Mexico.

The Buckeye One Butterfly is brown and orange, with big eyespots.

Zebra Longwing Butterfly: It lives in tropical areas in North America, the West Indies, Central and South America.

It is black with skinny yellow or white stripes and several red spots.

It has a bad taste, if eaten by predators.

It makes a loud cricking sound when it is in danger.

Paper Kite Butterfly: It lives in West Malaysia, Taiwan, and the Philippines. They live in tropical rainforests.

The butterfly is black and white (it really looks like it is made from paper!).

Tailed Jay Butterfly: It is a black butterfly with many green spots.

They can be found in India, Sri Lanka, Southeast Asia, and Australia.

Doris Longwing Butterfly: The background of this butterfly is black with a patch of color either red, blue, orange, or dark cream.

They live in Central America and the Amazon Rainforest.

The Doris Longwing Butterfly lives up to 9 months and it eats pollen and nectar.

Butterfly Meaning in Different Cultures

These are some of the meanings people believe butterflies have.

Ancient Romans believed butterflies were broken flowers.

In Japan, butterflies mean happiness and joy. To see a butterfly in a Japan is sign of good luck.

In Germany, they believe that the dead are reborn as children who fly as butterflies.

Greeks believed a new human was born each time a butterfly escaped from his/her chrysalis.

In China, seeing two butterflies flying together means love and long life.

Butterfly Facts

The fastest butterfly is the Skipper Butterfly. It can fly at 37 miles per hour.

Most butterflies fly about 5 to 12 miles per hour.

Butterflies are cold-blooded animals. They need sun to fly.

A group of butterflies is called a "Flutter."
In Pacific Groove, California there is a butterfly themed parade.

Butterflies cannot hear they just feel vibrations.

Conclusion

There are many places where you can go to watch butterflies and learn more about them.

Ask your parents to take you, now that you have read this book about butterflies.

Amazing Animal Book Series

My First Book About Butterflies   Page 37

My First Book About Butterflies　　　　　　　　　　　　　　　　　　　　Page 38

My First Book About Butterflies

My First Book About Butterflies   Page 40

My First Book About Butterflies

Our books are available at

1. Amazon.com

2. Barnes and Noble

3. Itunes

4. Kobo

5. Smashwords

6. Google Play Books

Download Free Books!
http://MendonCottageBooks.com

Publisher

JD-Biz Corp

P O Box 374

Mendon, Utah 84325

http://www.jd-biz.com/

Made in the USA
Monee, IL
25 November 2020